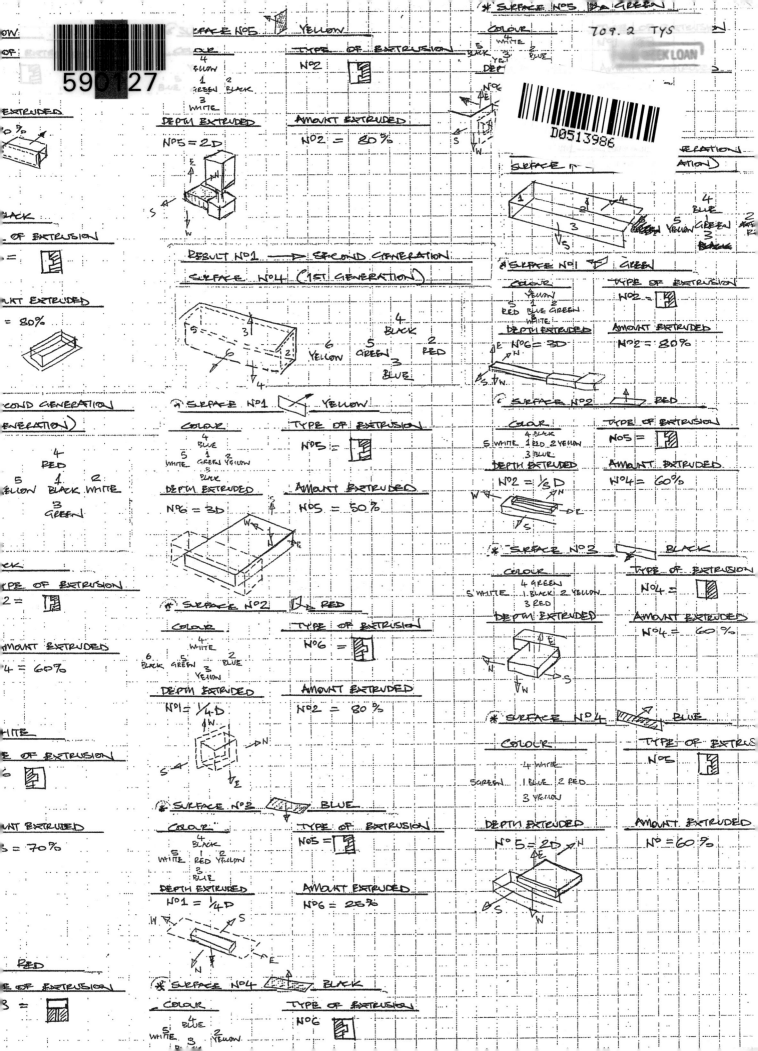

* SURFACE N°5 IS GREEN

SURFACE N°5   YELLOW

COLOUR
4 WHITE
5 BLACK   3 BLUE
YELLOW

709.2 TYS

COLOUR
4 YELLOW
1 GREEN   2 BLACK
3 WHITE

TYPE OF EXTRUSION
N°2 =

DEPTH EXTRUDED
N°5 = 2D

AMOUNT EXTRUDED
N°2 = 80%

EXTRUDED

BLACK

OF EXTRUSION
=

KT EXTRUDED
= 80%

SURFACE F

RESULT N°1 → SECOND GENERATION

SURFACE N°4 (1ST GENERATION)

4 BLACK
6 YELLOW   5 GREEN   2 RED
3 BLUE

* SURFACE N°1   GREEN

COLOUR
5 RED   1 YELLOW   2 GREEN
BLUE
WHITE

TYPE OF EXTRUSION
N°2 =

DEPTH EXTRUDED
N°6 = 3D

AMOUNT EXTRUDED
N°2 = 80%

COND GENERATION
ENERATION)

4 RED
5 YELLOW 1 BLACK 2 WHITE
3 GREEN

* SURFACE N°1   YELLOW

COLOUR
4 BLUE
5 WHITE 1 GREEN 2 YELLOW
3 BLACK

TYPE OF EXTRUSION
N°5 =

DEPTH EXTRUDED
N°6 = 3D

AMOUNT EXTRUDED
N°5 = 50%

C SURFACE N°2   RED

COLOUR
4 BLACK
5 WHITE 1 RED 2 YELLOW
3 BLUE

TYPE OF EXTRUSION
N°5 =

DEPTH EXTRUDED
N°2 = 1/3 D

AMOUNT EXTRUDED
N°4 = 60%

PE OF EXTRUSION
2 =

MOUNT EXTRUDED
4 = 60%

HITE

E OF EXTRUSION
6

* SURFACE N°2   RED

COLOUR
4 WHITE
6 BLACK 5 GREEN 2 BLUE
3 YELLOW

TYPE OF EXTRUSION
N°6 =

DEPTH EXTRUDED
N°1 = 1/4 D

AMOUNT EXTRUDED
N°2 = 80%

* SURFACE N°2   BLACK

COLOUR
4 GREEN
5 WHITE 1 BLACK 2 YELLOW
3 RED

TYPE OF EXTRUSION
N°4 =

DEPTH EXTRUDED

AMOUNT EXTRUDED
N°4 = 60%

* SURFACE N°4   BLUE

COLOUR
4 WHITE
5 GREEN 1 BLUE 2 RED
3 YELLOW

TYPE OF EXTRUS
N°

DEPTH EXTRUDED
N°5 = 2D

AMOUNT EXTRUDED
N° = 60%

NT EXTRUDED
= 70%

* SURFACE N°2   BLUE

COLOUR
4 BLACK
5 WHITE 1 RED 2 YELLOW
3 BLUE

TYPE OF EXTRUSION
N°5 =

DEPTH EXTRUDED
N°1 = 1/4 D

AMOUNT EXTRUDED
N°6 = 25%

RED

E OF EXTRUSION
3 =

* SURFACE N°4   BLACK

COLOUR
4 BLUE
5 WHITE 3 2 YELLOW

TYPE OF EXTRUSION
N°6

FRACTAL DICE

KEITH TYSON

FRACTAL DICE

September 5 – October 4, 2008

PACEWILDENSTEIN

545 West 22nd Street NYC 10011

Rule 1: Roll determines colors

4 = blue; 5 = yellow; 1 = red

Rule 2: Roll determines percent of face to be affected

5 = 50%

Rule 3: Roll determines type of extrusion

5 = right side, extending outward

Rule 4: Roll determines depth of extrusion

6 = three times the length of a side

Rule 1: Roll determines colors

6 = green; 5 = yellow; 4 = blue

On A Roll

By Marc Glimcher

In 2004 Keith Tyson began a series of works he entitled *Geno-Pheno*, short for Genotype-Phenotype. Like most of Tyson's projects, the works were constructed around a logical proposition, designed to illuminate certain aspects of "causality." These paintings were composed of two panels of identical size: the left side (Genotype) was a set or system with the potential to generate numerous results, while the right side was one of those results (Phenotype). For instance: on the left, a list of several dozen randomly selected words and, on the right, an elaborate image concocted from six of those words, chosen at random from the larger list. In a second example, on the left, a grid with a dozen or so points selected, each with an angle, a color, and number of seconds noted next to those points; on the right, an amorphous form of paint generated by pouring the designated color, at the designated angle, onto the panel for the designated amount of time.

More generally, any pluripotential system can be said to be a genotype from which one of many possible phenotypes might result. Even a six-sided die is a valid example. Such an object holds a genotype of six possible numbers but, once rolled, will express just one of those numbers as its phenotype.

FRACTAL DICE

The last group of *Geno-Pheno* works produced by Tyson was a series of sculptures made using the same organizing principles. These works utilized what Tyson loosely defined as a "base" to provide the genotype. The work which flowered from the generative system of that base (often consuming it) was the phenotype. For the current series, Tyson has returned to one of these sculptures, the *Fractal Die*, creating a series that uses the same methodology as the original. The works are made according to a mathematical system known as a random Iterative Function System, and then fabricated in three dimensions. An Iterative Function System is a set of rules or equations which are applied to some

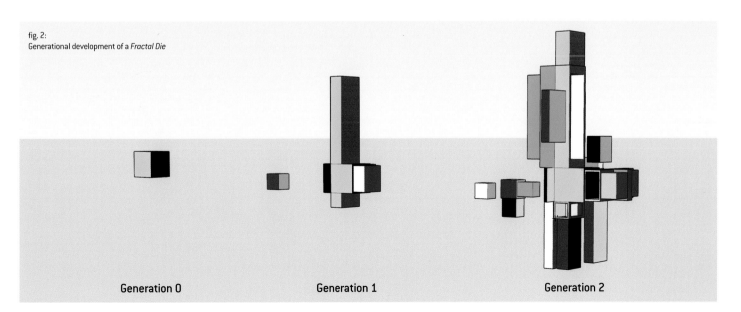

fig. 2:
Generational development of a *Fractal Die*

Generation 0   Generation 1   Generation 2

fig. 3:
Ripples of sand on a beach

fig. 4:
Five meter high sand dunes in
the Namibian Desert

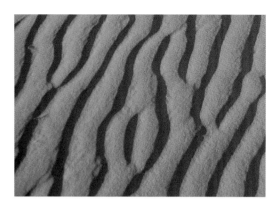

fig. 3:
Ripples of sand on a beach

fig. 4:
Five meter high sand dunes in
the Namibian Desert

original system. When applied, these rules alter that system in some way, creating a new form or "generation." The rules are then applied to the new form, creating the next generation. This iterative process continues for as many generations as the function specifies. The Iterative Function System is said to be random if the rules include variables which have values assigned by dice or some other kind of random number generator.

In the case of the *Fractal Dice*, Tyson has generated an Iterative Function System governing the transformation of each face of a simple cube. The rules governing those transformations include values determined by the roll of the die (fig. 1). The system progresses for two generations and is then fabricated in three dimensions (fig. 2).

Tyson's rules basically concern the generation of extensions or intrusions of different sizes, lengths and colors, depending on the roll of the die. As the function system proceeds, perhaps the most noticeable characteristic of the second generation is that the level of complexity seems far more than twice that of the first generation. Extrusions and intrusions cut and slice through each other, creating a tangle of elements caught in each others' grasp. Areas with small elements always appear highly intricate and complex. On the other hand, the long segments are relatively simple. Furthermore, the final sculptures take on the appearance of being long and skinny, with a mass of complicated elements closer to one end than the other.

None of these characteristics can be found in the rules. Just as there is no way to infer or calculate the numbers that will be generated by the 145 rolls of the die required for each sculpture, the *Fractal Dice* had to be made to reveal their qualities. This behavior of certain systems, as they proceed from Genotype to Phenotype, is of great interest to Tyson; when unpredictable forces and sets of simple rules are allowed to act on many similar objects over multiple generations, a phenomenon emerges known as complexity.

COMPLEXITY

Theoretically, there are simple processes and complex processes. An example of simple process is the flight of a cannonball. The angle of the cannon, the initial speed of the cannonball, and the force of gravity is all the information required to plot its precise trajectory. As a result, the point of impact can be plotted long before the cannon is fired.

In a complex process, none of these assumptions can be made. Take the example of sand dunes generated by wind blowing across the desert. Each sand grain is subject to a number of simple rules: gravity, wind resistance, momentum. The rules (which are not so different from the ones governing the cannonball) are then conditioned by the interaction of enormous numbers of individual elements, as well as their variety of shapes. These are the kinds of conditions that initiate complexity. In turn, complexity generates a specific set of characteristics which can be observed in systems as diverse as the weather or the stock market.

Unlike the cannonball, the movement of the sand is mathematically impossible to predict. And yet, wind-blown sand (and all complex systems) is observed to adopt certain highly consistent forms, namely the form of sand dunes. Furthermore, these forms are said to be self-similar, meaning 2-inch high ripples on the beach (fig. 3) have the same basic form as 20-meter high dunes in the Sahara (fig. 4).

FRACTALS

The quantification of these systems has presented a major challenge to modern mathematics. Euclidean geometry, for centuries, has measured the world using graphs and equations of one-, two-, or three-dimensional space. Fractal geometry measures complex forms and phenomena by gauging how far the system moves from one to two dimensions or from two to three dimensions. Imagine a line moving randomly across this page (the line is said to be one-dimensional and the plane of the sheet of paper is two-dimensional). The more complex it becomes, the more closely the line, coursing back and forth over itself, approximates the plane of the page. The closer the line comes to filling the two-dimensional page, the more closely its fractal value will approach 2 (figs. 5 and 6). This represents a fundamentally different approach to geometry and the concepts that have guided mathematics since Classical times. It is an approach that allows the investigation of all manner of complex systems to proceed in earnest.

For artists, such non-linear tools represent a significant closing of the gap between their work and modern mathematics. In fact, the landscape and phenomenology of complex systems has been fertile territory for artists for centuries. Their well-established use of foundational systems (for instance, the golden section) and their simultaneous embrace of "inspiration" represent, perhaps, the first human experimentation with complexity. This essay will seek to frame Tyson's current work in light of both art history and mathematical advances, illustrating how the mechanisms of his transformations engage these fundamental principles.

CASE STUDY #1: BOB ROSS

From 1983 until his untimely death in 1995, Bob Ross, a mechanic by training, was one of America's beloved and most famous artists[1]. His fame was not the result of museum exhibitions or spectacular auction results, but rather his highly rated afternoon Public Television series, "The Joy of Painting." Watched by millions throughout the world, the show would follow Ross as he went from a blank canvas to a pastoral scene of mountains or woodlands in a matter of thirty minutes. During the process, he would teach the viewers the "Bob Ross Method." Each step was codified and simplified and taught with the assurance that anyone could learn to paint.

The paintings themselves and Bob Ross in general came to be reviled by many in the art world. However, for the purposes of this analysis, Ross, his opinions, and the quality of the finished paintings are irrelevant. We will examine only the experience of those who watched and enjoyed his show.

As an oil painter, his technique and results may have been unremarkable, but for a non-artist, watching the image develop is a powerful experience. Ross realized this and the success of his program was due to the viewer's opportunity to watch a painting take shape, from start to finish. He was a master at heightening the experience, his soft soothing voice never rising above the action on the canvas surface. Just before the decisive moment, the camera would push in as Ross prepared his tools, palette knife, or fan brush for mountains and trees, respectively. The audience would see, for instance, a thin roll of titanium white paint, ready for delivery to the developing image and then, with only a fraction more flourish, the paint was applied. Instantaneously, the shadow-like form that had been waiting on the canvas became a mountain or a tree. Transformation was so complete and so sudden that the viewers' immediate reaction was a desire to see it again. When the palette knife delivered the white patch to the black form, the speed with which one's memories and associations of mountains exploded in the viewer's mind was too sudden to perceive.

Ross's twelve years of consistent ratings (including continued success in the years since his death) and passionate followers demonstrate that the moment of transformation does not "get old." Ross was delivering one of the key ingredients of art to a mass audience, the application of simple rules to create complexity. Allowing that transformation to persist in the finished work of art is a more difficult matter. But one should not underestimate how many appetites for art were whet by Bob Ross and his moments of transformation.

CASE STUDY #2: THE TREE

Bob Ross, or any artist for that matter, creates and utilizes systems which have the potential to become complex. One reason for this interest is the phenomenon of "naturalistic" images. It has been suggested that our ability to discriminate between natural and artificial may be due to an ability to perceive how complex an image is or perhaps even judge its fractal geometry compared to similar images found in nature. Think how quickly one can distinguish a "real" from a "fake" flower or tree. Artists have, over the past ten centuries, carefully probed these issues. Some have sought to simplify the complexity observed in nature, but for many historical lineages of artists, one can observe steady progress in their efforts to portray, or perhaps generate, complexity.

We will take the example of the tree. The tree is a classic example of a fractal system. Trees adopt complex, but highly recognizable forms. They demonstrate self-similarity; a 12-inch tangle of branches is difficult to distinguish from a 12-foot tangle on the same tree. And finally, they are the result of a few simple rules interacting with a few external elements: the sun, the wind, and the rain. Although there are certainly other factors, these are the major ones. The genetic programming of the cells that make up the living tissue on the tree can be simulated (again, highly simplified) with a few rules in an Iterative Function System, not unlike the *Fractal Dice*, and the results are computer-generated, reasonable facsimiles of trees.

Realizing that the mathematical systems necessary to generate these trees have only been with us since the 1960s, observe artists' efforts, over the centuries, to master the tree.

Early attempts focused on taming the image of the tree. Artists of the Middle Ages and the Renaissance took the elements of the tree, leaves, branches, and trunk, and gave them order and symmetry, generating the kind of stylized images we associate with those periods. But starting with the Baroque Italian masters, the well-known trend toward naturalism represents, in fact, the artists' early successes with complexity. Among the most impressive breakthroughs in this regard is that of Rembrandt. (Fellow Dutch master Johannes Vermeer achieved equal or perhaps greater feats of reproducing the complexity of the natural world; however, his techniques for doing so are as difficult to decode as Rembrandt's are obvious).

Look closely at Rembrandt's etching of a tree on a hill (fig. 7 and p. 10 [6]). The foliage of the tree is made up of an enormous number of very similar slashes and hook-shaped marks. This technique can be seen in hundreds of the master's etchings, engravings, and drawings. Rather than attempt to depict the forms that make up the tree, he depicts the process that makes up a tree. The result is instantly recognizable as more naturalistic than the more detailed trees of earlier periods. Rembrandt's advance is an advance not just in aesthetics but in our understanding of the nature of the complex systems that make up the real world. The work of J.M.W. Turner and later of the Impressionists would further expand artists' process-oriented, visual understanding of complexity.

fig. 7:
Rembrandt Harmensz van Rijn
Landscape with Three Trees (detail)
1643
Etching with drypoint and engraving
8 3/8 x 11 1/8"
Musée Condé, Chantilly, France

10

[1] *Lion attacking antelopes under a tree*
Umayyad dynasty, c. 710–50
Mosaic of the bath
Khirbat al-Mafjar, Israel

[2] **Fra Angelico**
Cella 1: Noli me tangere; Christ meets Mary Magdalen in the garden, 1438
Mural, 65 3/8 x 49 1/4"
Museo di S. Marco, Florence

[3] **Leonardo da Vinci**
The Annunciation (detail), c. 1472–75
Tempera on wood, 38 1/2 x 85 3/8"
Uffizi, Florence

[4] **Michelangelo Merisi da Caravaggio**
On the Road to Calvary (detail), c. 1533
Oil on wood, 51 1/4 x 97 1/4"
Museo e Gallerie Nazionali di Capodimonte, Naples

[5] **Gian Lorenzo Bernini**
Apollo and Daphne (detail), 1622–25
Carrara marble, 9' 3/4"
Galleria Borghese, Rome

[6] **Rembrandt Harmensz van Rijn**
Landscape with Three Trees (detail), 1643
Etching with drypoint and engraving
8 3/8 x 11 1/8"
Musée Condé, Chantilly, France

[7] **Georges Seurat**
Study for Sunday Afternoon on the Island of the Grande Jatte (detail), 1884
Oil on wood, 6 1/8 x 9 1/2"
The Metropolitan Museum of Art, New York;
Robert Lehman Collection

[8] **Claude Monet**
Poplars on the Bank of the Epte River (detail), 1891
Oil on canvas, 39 1/2 x 25 11/16"
Philadelphia Museum of Art, Pennsylvania;
Bequest of Anne Thomson in memory of her father, Frank Thomson, and her mother, Mary Elizabeth Clarke Thomson

[9] **Georges Braque**
Viaduct at L'Estaque (detail), 1908
Oil on canvas, 28 1/2 x 23 1/4"
Musée National d'Art Moderne, Centre Georges Pompidou, Paris

[10] **Piet Mondrian**
"The Tree A", 1913
Oil on canvas, 39 1/2 x 26 1/2"
Tate Gallery, London; Purchased 1977
© 2008 Mondrian/Holtzman Trust c/o HCR International, Warrenton, Virginia

[11] **Alexander Calder**
Bougainvillier (Bougainvillea), 1947
Sheet metal, wire, rod, lead, and paint
78 1/2 x 86"

[12] **Agnes Martin**
The Tree, 1964
Oil and pencil on canvas, 72 x 72"
The Museum of Modern Art, New York;
Larry Aldrich Foundation Fund

[4]

[1]

[5]

[2]

[6]

[3]

[7]

[10]

[8]

[11]

[9]

[12]

In the twentieth century, artists continued to explore how complexity could be captured. They experimented by removing elements of the tree, while attempting to preserve its nature, as in the Mondrian (p. 11 [10]). The final image of a "tree" is a 1964 painting by abstract artist Agnes Martin (fig. 8 and p. 11 [12]). After years of creating vaguely biomorphic paintings, Martin began painting strictly geometric systems, pencil grids, or lines, suspended on or in fields of mostly uniform color.

> A lot of people say my work is like landscape. But the truth is that it isn't, because there are straight lines in my work and there are no straight lines in nature. My work is non-objective, like that of the abstract expressionists. But I want people, when they look at my paintings, to have the same feelings they experience when they look at landscape so I never protest when they say my work is like landscape. But it's really about the feeling of beauty and freedom that you experience in landscape. I would say that my response to nature is really a response to beauty. The water looks beautiful, the trees look beautiful. It is beauty that really calls.[2]

To all appearances, she was rejecting the complexity of the natural system in favor of an idealized one. Indeed, she often referred to Greek Classicism and Platonic ideals as the realm she hoped her work would occupy. If ever there was a painter who seemed the natural defender Euclidean geometry, she would be the one. However, there is much more to her work than right angles and simplification. As the quotation above shows, her primary interest was perfection and the perception of perfection, which she claimed to be beauty. From the standpoint of complexity and causality, we must ask how Martin drew her conclusions about perfection. Was she recognizing some ideal state of perfection, defining it as beautiful and then learning to derive a sort of abstract version? Or rather, was she observing beauty in the world and thereby defining those objects as having some measure of perfection? Clearly the latter, and although she "painted with her back to the world," she was informed by her observation of and belief in beauty in the natural world. To Martin, *The Tree* was the crystallization of the tree's beauty and perfection. The grid on the canvas was the very real residue of the thing that made the tree beautiful. If such paintings are, in some sense, related to the nature of complex objects, is the converse also true? Could we say that the simple grid was Martin's intuitive manifestation of the simple systems which generate the tree in all its all complex glory? Even the titles of her early paintings suggest an interest in the simple systems which complexity theory has used to demonstrate these principles: *The Night Sea, Dune, Wheat Field, The Peach, Islands, Grey Stone* and *Leaf in the Wind*.

fig. 9
Jackson Pollock
Autumn Rhythm (Number 30), 1950
Enamel on canvas, 105 x 207"
The Metropolitan Museum of Art, New York;
George A. Hearn Fund

fig. 10
Jackson Pollock, 1950
Photograph by Hans Namuth

CASE STUDY #3: JACKSON POLLOCK

>…method is, it seems to me, a natural growth out of a need, and from a need the
>modern artist has found new ways of expressing the world about him. I happen to
>find ways that are different from the usual techniques of painting, which seems a little
>strange at the moment, but I don't think there's anything very different about it… .[3]

In the late 1940s, Jackson Pollock became one of the most famous artists in history. His painting had evolved from semi-abstract surrealist compositions to fully abstract canvases, using nothing more than splatters and drips of paint as content (fig. 9). Despite the renown of these abstractions, Pollock's methods remain unknown to all but the most dedicated students of his work. Yet, understanding these methods is crucial to understanding how he used the phenomenon of complexity to create his work.

Pollock's drip paintings are not the result of wild, uncontrolled release or some semi-conscious altered state. Rather, they are the result of a carefully choreographed process where the freely falling paint is brought together on the canvas using a number of well-developed processes.

The misconception that Pollock slung paint in a fit of rage is tied to a belief that such behavior, like a tantric state, unlocks some hidden realm. But signs of chaos[4] are mostly absent from the work. Instead, the skeins of paint result from a purposeful system of directionality and layering. The care with which Pollock attends his program is abundantly clear from the famous films shot by Hans Namuth in 1950 (fig. 10).

Pollock's paintings are, in fact, a true complex system of the artist's own creation. They are not a replication of an observed system like a mountain or a river, but something new, generated by his rules and the physical events he subjects them to. Furthermore, the nature of those rules and of his approach is such that, in the end, the paintings share certain qualities with the mountains and the rivers, just as mountains and rivers share certain qualities in common with each other. Those qualities are the ones which we can loosely define as fractal or complex.

In academic circles, much has been made of Pollock's deft use of complex systems. In 1999, Dr. Richard Taylor of the Department of Physics, University of Oregon (Eugene), published the first of many papers documenting the fractal analysis of Pollock's drip paintings.[5] The details of the fractal geometry of Pollock's work have become a favorite topic for first year math and physics graduate students (especially when drip paintings of questionable authenticity appear on the art market and auction houses start calling mathematics departments for help). Considerable research has demonstrated that in some paintings Pollock did, in fact, achieve a highly unusual level of fractal geometry. The research claims that Pollock generated a level of complexity in the paintings that is rarely observed in a man-made object. These researchers go on to suggest that this unique aspect of the work, one shared by "natural" complex systems, is the reason for the work's influence and success. They extend the argument by hypothesizing that humans might have some innate positive response to such fractal systems, and that the recognition of such systems almost certainly confers some greater level of Darwinian fitness on the individual possessing it, and that a careful study might reveal the very meaning and purpose of art itself.

Whatever the implications, the powerful and deeply satisfying sensation of looking at the matrix of interweaving lines and splatters that make up a Pollock is apparent to most observers. Only a few minutes in the presence of one of these paintings makes it clear that the artist kept at his simple process long enough and with enough discipline to allow something powerful to emerge. It is not hard to imagine the moment of metamorphosis as the layers of the skeins built up. Like a fire-stick being turned in a clump of dry grass, first a curl of smoke, then a crackle, and suddenly the fuel bursts into flame. At some crucial moment, the system hits a critical level of complexity and the Pollock catches fire for the artist or any viewer fortunate enough to be present.

THE NEXT GENERATION

The few examples cited above illustrate both the nature of complex systems and some ways in which they have permeated the art-making process. Tyson's experiment demonstrates those elements in action: simple rules driven by the engine of chance (the basic ingredients of complexity). The results are sculptures that display relatedness to each other (adopting forms), while preserving their individual uniqueness (unpredictability), characteristics typical of any group of artworks. This may seem like a trivial accomplishment, but it is not. If one attempted to write a computer program that would create a group a works which demonstrated these characteristics through the use of commands and descriptions (rather than the simple rules and dice rolls Tyson employed), it would require thousands of hours and the services of a super-computer. Even with powerful computing methods, the lack of inherent complexity would make the sculpture look "fake" compared to the *Fractal Dice*. This is the starting point for Tyson, because the *Fractal Dice* go far beyond codifying complexity in the process of artmaking. They seek to reveal the hidden side of that process in a new way.

THE PROBABILISTIC LANDSCAPE

A set of rules is applied again and again to the same starting conditions. The result is that the object will "grow" or "change" in height, width, and depth. As the rules are applied to successive generations, these changes occur over "time" (see fig 1). Such a phenomenon is referred to as four-dimensional because it involves the three dimensions of space (height, width, depth) and change over time, the fourth dimension. Tyson's *Fractal Dice*, however, add a fifth dimension to this array: probability. All possible rolls of the die create a set of possible forms that the sculpture could take and the probability that they would occur.[6] He imagines these ranges of possibilities to be a kind of landscape that expresses the complete nature of the work. From this perspective, the roll of the die does not create the sculpture, rather it acts as an instrument to locate one point on that landscape and allow the artist to make it visible. Pollock, like many artists of his generation, saw himself as accessing some invisible, inner world. Tyson's system locates a similarly invisible world. He describes the *Fractal Dice* as an intersection between the viewer and this probabilistic landscape. Can the mathematical iterations of Tyson's approach connect with Pollock's Freudian/Jungian "interior" world? If Tyson is correct, it is the act of creating such an intersection between the viewer and some hidden system that all artists share.

While Tyson employs the tools of scientific and logical inquiry when making his work, and does so with powerful results, they are just that—tools, no different from those used by artists from Rembrandt to Bob Ross. The *Fractal Dice*, like any painting by Agnes Martin, was designed to use the fewest possible variables, to produce the unmistakable experience of complexity and of the experience of complex systems in the "real world." Tyson's *Fractal Dice* do not resemble trees any more than Martin's canvas does, and yet both works may say more about what it means to experience a tree than any attempt to replicate its image. Tyson's desire is to "reveal the experience of living in this universe." The *Fractal Dice* are one more step in his ongoing efforts to discover new routes to those hidden provinces.

Endnotes

1. For more information on Bob Ross, please see www.bobross.com.

2. Quoted in Irving Sandler, "Agnes Martin," *Art Monthly* 169 (September 1993), p. 3–11.

3. Jackson Pollock, interview with William Wright, The Springs, Long Island, New York, late 1950. Broadcast on radio station WERI, Westerly, Rhode Island, 1951.

4. Chaos is a mathematical state distinct from complexity. Like complexity, it creates unpredictable results, but the system's underlying patterns are entirely absent.

5. Taylor, Richard. "Fractal Analysis of Pollock's Drip Paintings." *Nature* 399 (1999), p. 422.

6. As a result of the details of the rules, some of the millions of possible forms are more likely to occur than others.

Geno Pheno Sculpture:

FRACTAL DICE NO. 1

2005

aluminum and plastic

3' x 17' 8" x 3' 9"

914 x 5385 x 1143 mm

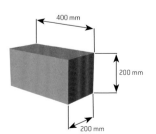

Starting Condition

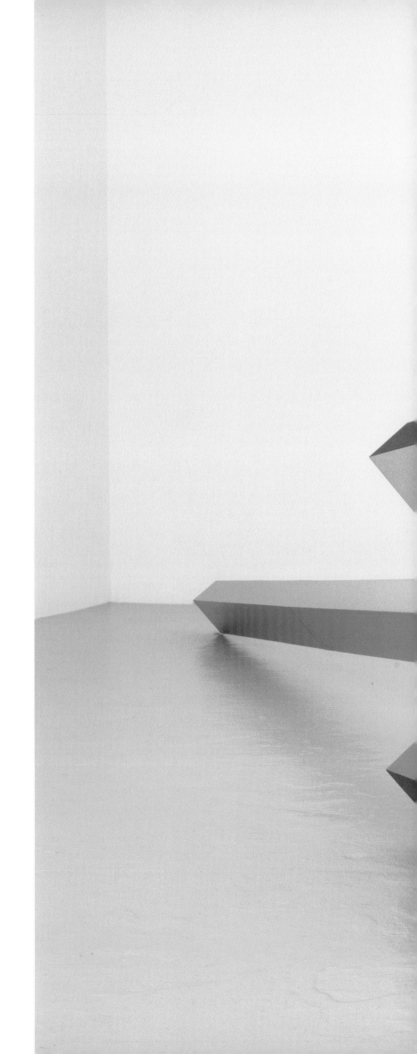

Fractal Die:

FIRST ROLL

2005–08

aluminum and plastic

5' 9 1/8" x 3' 3 3/8" x 9' 2 3/8"

1756 x 1000 x 2804 mm

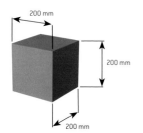

Starting Condition

Fractal Die:

SECOND ROLL

2005–08

aluminum and plastic

2' 10 1/2" x 9' 2 1/2" x 5' 9"

876 x 2807 x 1753 mm

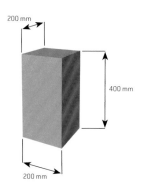

Starting Condition

Fractal Die:

THIRD ROLL

2005–08

aluminum and plastic

2' x 9' 8 ¹/₂" x 3' 7"

610 x 2959 x 1092 mm

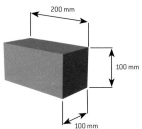

200 mm

100 mm

100 mm

Starting Condition

Fractal Die:

FOURTH ROLL

2005–08

aluminum and plastic

2' 8" x 5' 4" x 8' 3"

813 x 1626 x 2515 mm

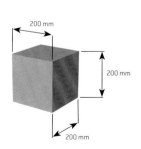

Starting Condition

Fractal Die:

FIFTH ROLL

2005–08

aluminum and plastic

2' 4" x 10' 8" x 8' 11"

711 x 3251 x 2718 mm

(In fabrication)

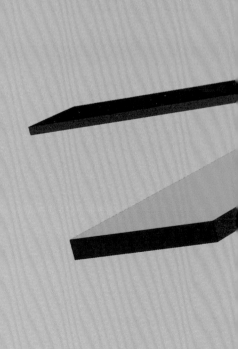

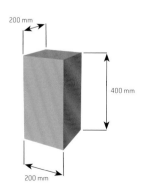

200 mm

400 mm

200 mm

Starting Condition

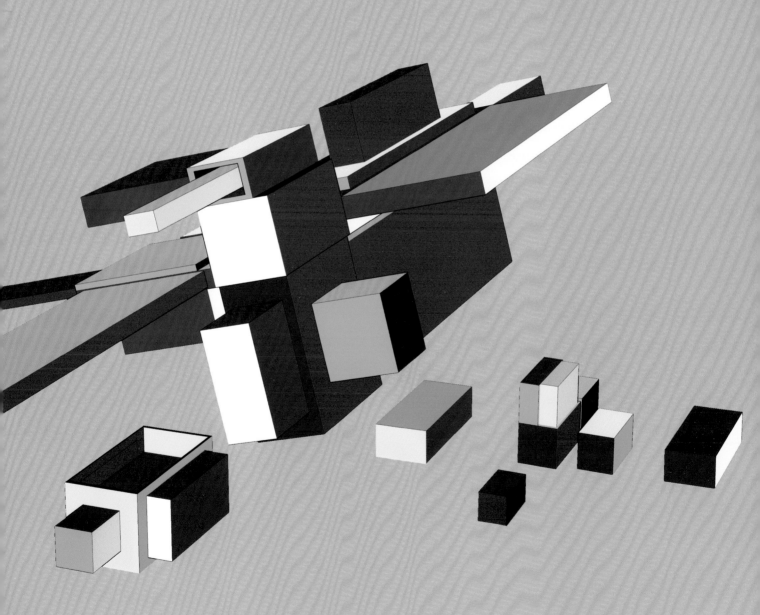

Fractal Die:

SIXTH ROLL

2005–08

aluminum and plastic

9' 4" x 7' 2" x 2' 7"

2845 x 2184 x 787 mm

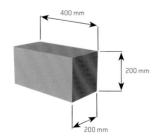

Starting Condition

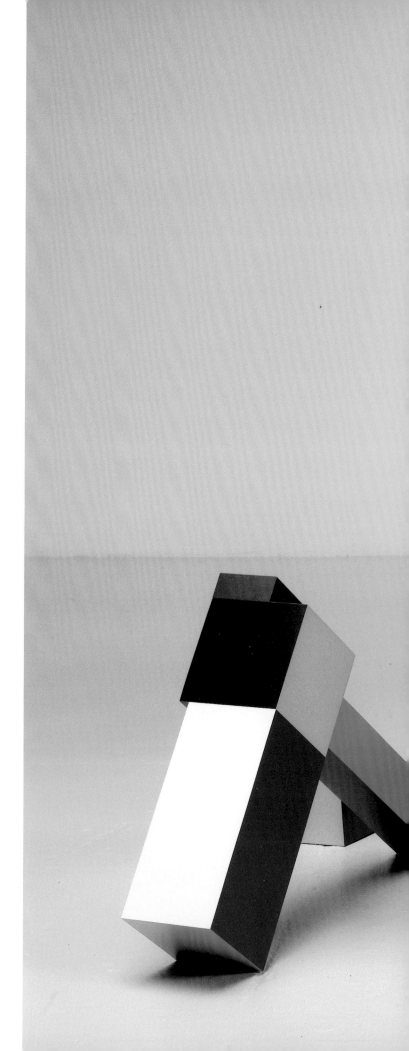

Fractal Die:

SEVENTH ROLL

2005–08

aluminum and plastic

29 $^1/_2$ x 44 $^1/_2$ x 31 $^7/_8$"

749 x 1130 x 810 mm

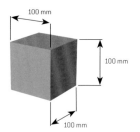

Starting Condition

Fractal Die:

EIGHTH ROLL

2005–08

aluminum and plastic

70 $^1/_2$ x 70 x 31 $^1/_2$"

1791 x 1778 x 800 mm

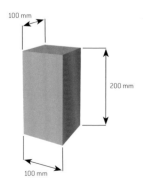

Starting Condition

Fractal Die:

NINTH ROLL

2005–08

aluminum and plastic

13 x 74 ¹/₂ x 67"

330 x 1892 x 1702 mm

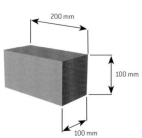

200 mm

100 mm

100 mm

Starting Condition

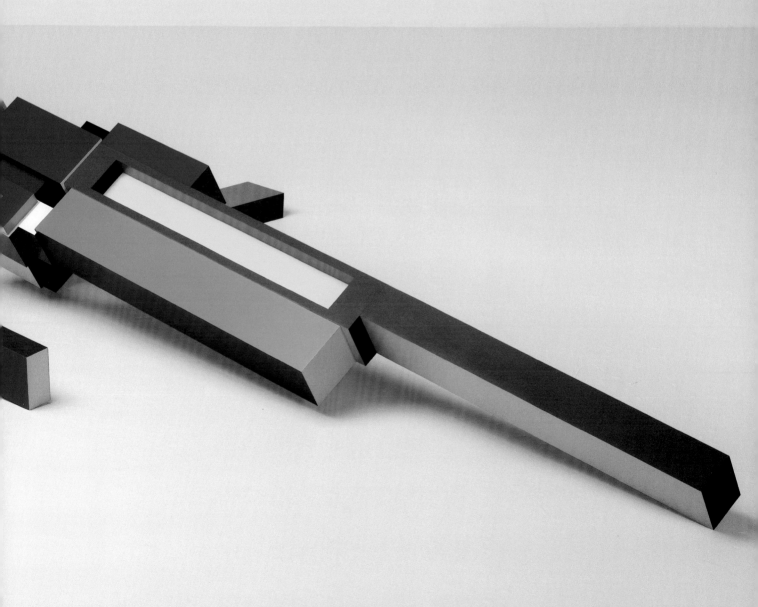

Fractal Die:

TENTH ROLL

2005–08

aluminum and plastic

29 x 16 $^1/_2$ x 29 $^1/_2$"

737 x 419 x 749 mm

(In fabrication)

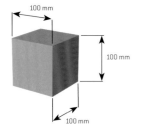

Starting Condition

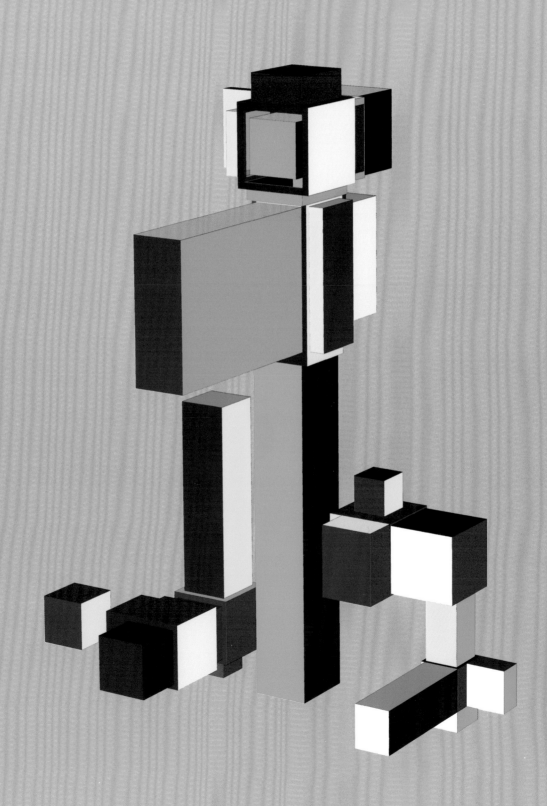

Fractal Die:

ELEVENTH ROLL

2005–08

aluminum and plastic

36 x 37 x 45 1/2"

914 x 940 x 1156 mm

(In fabrication)

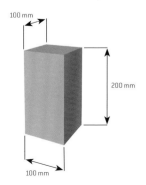

100 mm

200 mm

100 mm

Starting Condition

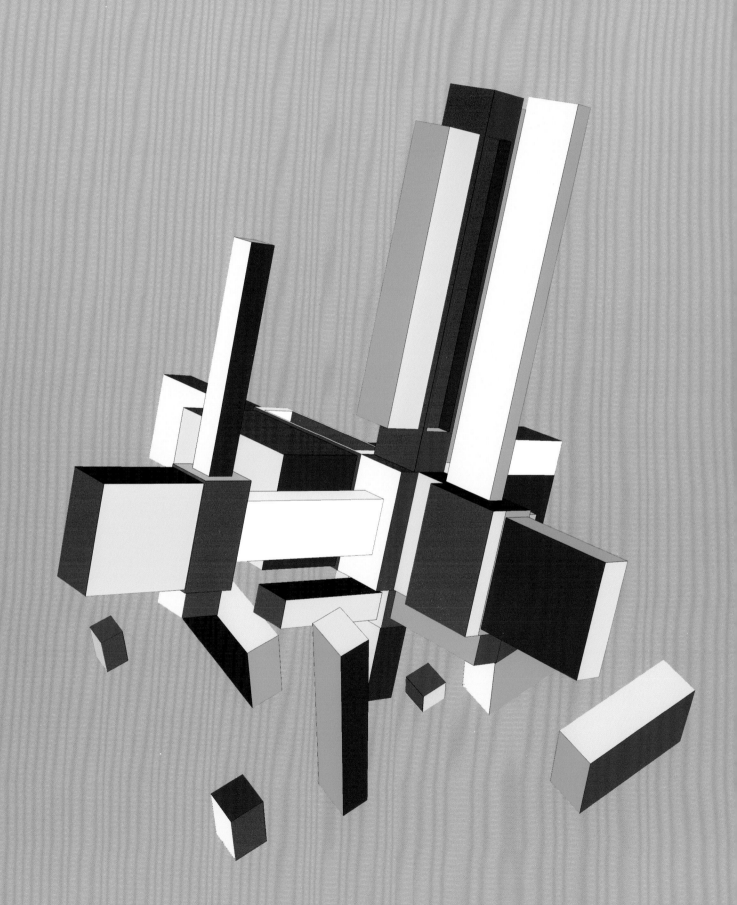

Fractal Die:

FOURTEENTH ROLL

2005–08

aluminum and plastic

8' ³/4" x 10' ¹/4" x 1' 4 ¹/2"

2457 x 3054 x 419 mm

(In fabrication)

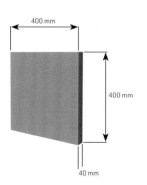

Starting Condition

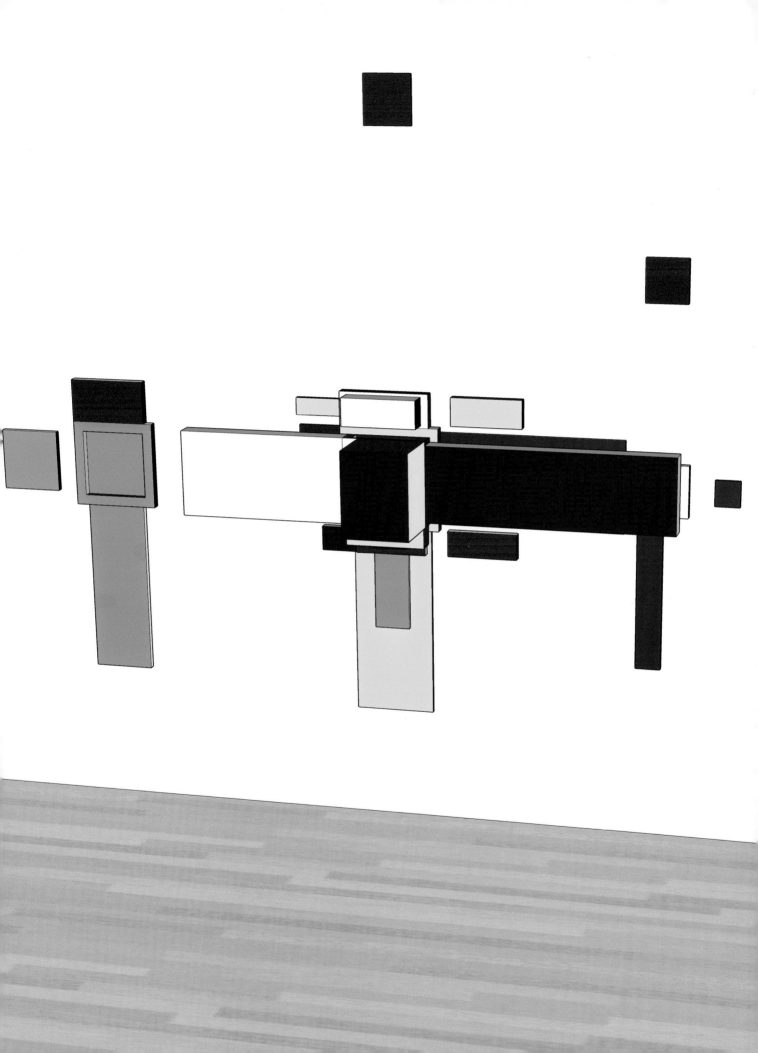

Fractal Die:

FIFTEENTH ROLL

2005–08

aluminum and plastic

14' x 7' 10 1/2" x 4 3/8"

4267 x 2400 x 111 mm

(In fabrication)

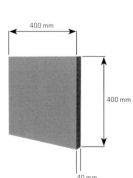

400 mm

400 mm

40 mm

Starting Condition

Checklist

SERIES	TITLE	YEAR	MATERIAL	DIMENSIONS, IMPERIAL	DIMENSIONS, METRIC
Geno Pheno Sculpture	FRACTAL DICE NO. 1	2005	aluminum and plastic	3' x 17' 8" x 3' 9"	914 x 5385 x 1143 mm
Fractal Die	FIRST ROLL	2005–08	aluminum and plastic	5' 9 $^1/_8$" x 3' 3 $^3/_8$" x 9' 2 $^3/_8$"	1756 x 1000 x 2804 mm
Fractal Die	SECOND ROLL	2005–08	aluminum and plastic	2' 10 $^1/_2$" x 9' 2 $^1/_2$" x 5' 9"	876 x 2807 x 1753 mm
Fractal Die	THIRD ROLL	2005–08	aluminum and plastic	2' x 9' 8 $^1/_2$" x 3' 7"	610 x 2959 x 1092 mm
Fractal Die	FOURTH ROLL	2005–08	aluminum and plastic	2' 8" x 5' 4" x 8' 3"	813 x 1626 x 2515 mm
Fractal Die	FIFTH ROLL	2005–08	aluminum and plastic	2' 4" x 10' 8" x 8' 11"	711 x 3251 x 2718 mm
Fractal Die	SIXTH ROLL	2005–08	aluminum and plastic	9' 4" x 7' 2" x 2' 7"	2845 x 2184 x 787 mm
Fractal Die	SEVENTH ROLL	2005–08	aluminum and plastic	29 $^1/_2$ x 44 $^1/_2$ x 31 $^7/_8$"	749 x 1130 x 810 mm
Fractal Die	EIGHTH ROLL	2005–08	aluminum and plastic	70 $^1/_2$ x 70 x 31 $^1/_2$"	1791 x 1778 x 800 mm
Fractal Die	NINTH ROLL	2005–08	aluminum and plastic	13 x 74 $^1/_2$ x 67"	330 x 1892 x 1702 mm
Fractal Die	TENTH ROLL	2005–08	aluminum and plastic	29 x 16 $^1/_2$ x 29 $^1/_2$"	737 x 419 x 749 mm
Fractal Die	ELEVENTH ROLL	2005–08	aluminum and plastic	36 x 37 x 45 $^1/_2$"	914 x 940 x 1156 mm
Fractal Die	FOURTEENTH ROLL	2005–08	aluminum and plastic	8' $^3/_4$" x 10' $^1/_4$" x 1' 4 $^1/_2$"	2457 x 3054 x 419 mm
Fractal Die	FIFTEENTH ROLL	2005–08	aluminum and plastic	14' x 7' 10 $^1/_2$" x 4 $^3/_8$"	4267 x 2400 x 111 mm

Catalogue © 2008 PaceWildenstein

Works of art by Keith Tyson © 2008 Keith Tyson

Work of art by Georges Braque © 2008 Artists Rights
Society (ARS), New York/ADAGP, Paris

Work of art by Alexander Calder © 2008 Calder Foundation,
New York/Artists Rights Society (ARS), New York

Text and work of art by Agnes Martin © 2008 Agnes Martin/
Artists Rights Society (ARS), New York

Work of art by Piet Mondrian © 2008 Mondrian/Holtzman
Trust c/o HCR International, Warrenton, Virginia.

Work of art by Jackson Pollock © 2008 The Pollock-Krasner
Foundation/Artists Rights Society (ARS), New York

Text by Marc Glimcher © 2008 Marc Glimcher

Photography:

Bill Bachman/Photo Researchers, Inc. © 2008 Photo
Researchers, Inc. All rights reserved; p. 6 (fig. 3)

The Bridgeman Art Library; p. 10 [4]

Courtesy Calder Foundation, New York; p. 11 [11]

G.R. Christmas; pp. 18–19, 22–25, 30–35

CNAC/MNAM/Dist. Réunion des Musées Nationaux/Art
Resource, NY; p. 11 [9]

Bernhard Edmaier/Photo Researchers, Inc. © 2008 Photo
Researchers, Inc. All rights reserved; p. 6 (fig. 4)

Dr. Fred Espenak/Photo Researchers, Inc. © 2008 Photo
Researchers, Inc. All rights reserved; p. 7 (fig. 6)

Giraudon/Art Resource, NY; pp. 9 (fig. 7), 10 [6]

Erich Lessing/Art Resource, NY; p. 10 [2]

Joerg Lohse; pp. 20–21

Mauro Magliani for Alinari/Art Resource, NY; p. 10 [5]

Kerry Ryan McFate; pp. 16–17, 28–29

© The Metropolitan Museum of Art, New York/Art
Resource, NY; pp. 11 [7], 13 (fig. 9)

© The Museum of Modern Art, New York/Licensed by
SCALA/Art Resource, NY; pp. 11 [12], 12 (fig. 8)

Hans Namuth © 1991 Hans Namuth Estate, courtesy Center
for Creative Photography, University of Arizona; p. 13 (fig. 10)

Alfred Pasieka/Photo Researchers, Inc. © 2008 Photo
Researchers, Inc. All rights reserved; p. 7 (fig. 5)

Philadelphia Museum of Art/Art Resource, NY; p. 11 [8]

SCALA/Art Resource, NY; p. 10 [1]

SCALA/Ministero per i Beni e le Attività culturali/Art
Resource, NY; p. 10 [3]

Tate, London/Art Resource, NY; p. 11 [10]

Design:
Tomo Makiura

Production:
PaceWildenstein

Color Correction:
Motohiko Tokuta

Printing:
Meridian Printing, East Greenwich, Rhode Island

Library of Congress Control Number: 2008934683
ISBN: 9781930743908

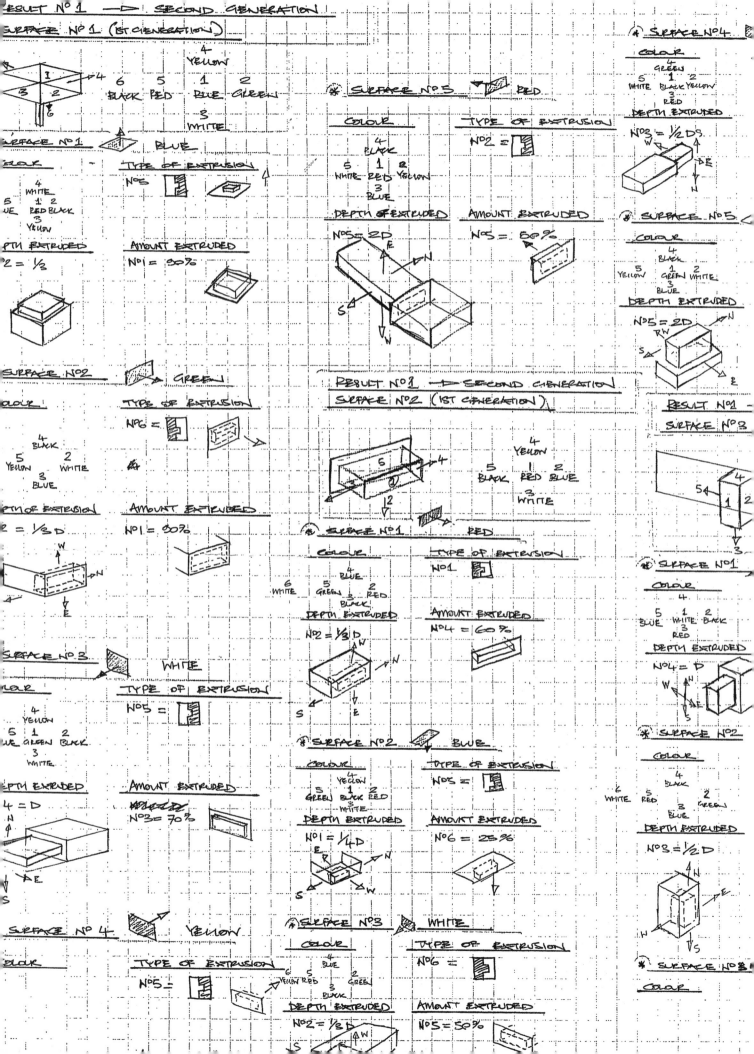

RESULT Nº 1 → SECOND GENERATION

SURFACE Nº 1 (1ST GENERATION)

4 YELLOW
6   5   1   2
BLACK RED BLUE GREEN
3 WHITE

SURFACE Nº 1 — BLUE

COLOUR
4 WHITE
5   1   2
BLUE RED BLACK
3 YELLOW

TYPE OF EXTRUSION
Nº6

DEPTH EXTRUDED
Nº2 = 1/3

AMOUNT EXTRUDED
Nº1 = 80%

SURFACE Nº2 — GREEN

COLOUR
4 BLACK
5   2
YELLOW WHITE
3 BLUE

TYPE OF EXTRUSION
Nº6 =

DEPTH OF EXTRUSION
Nº2 = 1/3 D

AMOUNT EXTRUDED
Nº1 = 80%

SURFACE Nº3 — WHITE

COLOUR
4 YELLOW
5   1
BLUE GREEN BLACK
3 WHITE

TYPE OF EXTRUSION
Nº5 =

DEPTH EXTRUDED
Nº4 = D

AMOUNT EXTRUDED
Nº3 = 70%

SURFACE Nº 4 — YELLOW

COLOUR
BLACK

TYPE OF EXTRUSION
Nº5 =

SURFACE Nº5 — RED

COLOUR
4 BLACK
5   1   2
WHITE RED YELLOW
3 BLUE

TYPE OF EXTRUSION
Nº2 =

DEPTH OF EXTRUDED
Nº5 = 2D

AMOUNT EXTRUDED
Nº5 = 50%

RESULT Nº 1 → SECOND GENERATION
SURFACE Nº 2 (1ST GENERATION)

4 YELLOW
5   1   2
BLACK RED BLUE
3 WHITE

SURFACE Nº1 — RED

COLOUR
4 BLUE
6   5   2
WHITE GREEN RED
3 BLACK

TYPE OF EXTRUSION
Nº1

DEPTH EXTRUDED
Nº2 = 1/3 D

AMOUNT EXTRUDED
Nº4 = 60%

SURFACE Nº2 — BLUE

COLOUR
4 YELLOW
5   1   2
GREEN BLACK RED
3 WHITE

TYPE OF EXTRUSION
Nº5 =

DEPTH EXTRUDED
Nº1 = 1/4 D

AMOUNT EXTRUDED
Nº6 = 25%

SURFACE Nº3 — WHITE

COLOUR
4 BLUE
6   5   2
YELLOW RED GREEN
3 BLACK

TYPE OF EXTRUSION
Nº6 =

DEPTH EXTRUDED
Nº2 = 1/3 D

AMOUNT EXTRUDED
Nº5 = 50%

SURFACE Nº4

COLOUR
4 GREEN
5   1   2
WHITE BLACK YELLOW
3 RED

DEPTH EXTRUDED
Nº3 = 1/2 DS.

SURFACE Nº5

COLOUR
4 BLACK
5   1   2
YELLOW GREEN WHITE
3 BLUE

DEPTH EXTRUDED
Nº5 = 2D

RESULT Nº 1 —
SURFACE Nº3

SURFACE Nº1

COLOUR
4
5   1   2
BLUE WHITE BLACK
3 RED

DEPTH EXTRUDED
Nº4 = D

SURFACE Nº2

COLOUR
4 BLACK
6   5   2
WHITE RED GREEN
3 BLUE

DEPTH EXTRUDED
Nº3 = 1/2 D

SURFACE Nº3

COLOUR